FIREFIGHTING
AND FAITH

FIREFIGHTING
AND FAITH

Mark W. McAdams

Xulon Press Elite

Xulon Press Elite
2301 Lucien Way #415
Maitland, FL 32751
407.339.4217
www.xulonpress.com

Paperback ISBN-13: 978-1-6628-2594-1
Ebook ISBN-13: 978-1-6628-2595-8

TABLE OF CONTENTS

FOREWORD

GROWING UP IN CENTRAL TEXAS IN A SMALL
*town, I was able to enjoy the benefits of a stable
family life and being raised in what we would have
called a "church-going family." I often look back
now at what I was taught about faith versus what
I have experienced and think that maybe there was
a bit of misdirection in my spiritual upbringing.
None of the misdirection was based in intentional
negligence, but I believe it was more founded in
a process of tradition versus development of a
relationship with God Himself.*

*In any case, I was unprepared on a spiritual
level to meet the world. Having grown up believing
that life would proceed along a natural course
of graduating high school, getting married and
having children while working in whatever job
availed itself, I had no idea of the challenges that
life would throw at me, let alone understand that
the biggest challenge was overcoming things that
resided within myself.*

In short, I quickly became "chewed up and spit out" when it came to dealing with life.

From a young age I struggled with self-esteem. I often wanted to blame a dad who was quick to criticize whatever I did, but I got over that. I learned it was something I needed to overcome. I became a pretty hard alcoholic by the age of fifteen, and also became pretty good at hiding it from the family. At the age of seventeen I quit school and joined the Navy for two hitches, and during this time my alcoholism, anger, and tendency to become violent grew.

Due to this I had the experience of being arrested in four countries by the time I was twenty-two, as well as doing some time in military incarceration, which we called "the brig" in the Navy.

I was lost, afraid, bitter and hopeless at a young age. I turned my back on God while all the time being sure He loved me and wanted me to come to Him. I have always been thankful for my parents who taught me of God and His mercy, although I had not truly understood it. I was under the impression that we were saved by grace, but we stayed that way by "toeing the line."

I was never one to "toe the line" very well. I believe they would call that rebellious.

Again, I had no idea that life would throw these challenges into the road before me, and I certainly never thought the greatest challenge would be dealing with my own demons.

Due to my rebellious, drunken and violent habits, at the age of twenty-three I had been court martialed for being on unauthorized absence from my duties, as well as assault charges. I was restricted to the ship I was assigned to, meaning I could not leave that ship as I waited for a spot to open up in the brig, where I had been sentenced to six months of incarceration. I was in a place that felt hopeless. And I now see that the enemy was doing a pretty good job at supporting that mindset in me.

There was a chief petty officer onboard who talked the captain into allowing me to go to his church as they were holding a week-long revival. Surprisingly, both the captain and I agreed. That chief petty officer was used by God more than he will ever know.

This gave me an opportunity to get off the ship in my mind. Little did I know that three nights later, I would come into a relationship with Jesus. You see, I knew about Jesus. Actually, with my religious upbringing I was somewhat knowledgeable about Holy Scripture. But that night I found out the difference between knowing **about** someone and **personally knowing** someone.

I miraculously received my second honorable discharge after doing my brig time, due to my hitch being completed. Three years later, I began my career as a firefighter, which I am convinced has been one of the greatest blessings God has given me. Becoming a firefighter proved to me that God truly does have a plan and a purpose for our lives.

I wish I could say that from there on in it was smooth sailing. But I cannot. I struggled with my own selfish desires and alcoholism for years to come. I experience divorce in my life and struggled with depression many times.

In the book of James, the author writes about how a doubting man is unstable in all his ways and is like wave of the sea that is tossed and driven by the wind. Well, I think that is an accurate description of my life in the faith for a long while. I was sure about my relationship with Jesus. I just was unwilling to commit myself fully to that relationship and trust Him in everything.

It was actually not until the age of forty-five that I truly surrendered myself to Jesus. But I see that He kept His word and never left me along the way.

As I said, the fire service was one of the greatest blessings God has given me to show His plan and *purpose for me. The brother firefighters, the calls we made, the lessons we learned, were all used by God to bring me to the realization that it is only with God that I won when I surrendered. For thirty-five years, reaching the rank of captain in a large metropolitan department and then moving on to be fire chief of two smaller departments, God showed me the way and allowed me to come closer to Him even though I took many exits and detours, following my own fears, selfishness and pride along the way.*

That chief petty officer in the Navy who cared enough to take me to a church meeting told me that God spoke in four ways. In prayer, in scripture, through people, and through life's circumstances. He was right.

I have been blessed to have served in the fire service with the most wonderful people. Through the victories, traumas, and failures, I have come to know the peace of God through Jesus Christ. And I finally realized that it was peace I was looking for all along. Even when I chose the counterfeit paths to find it.

I thank God for being faithful and never leaving or forsaking me. I thank Him for always having His arms open to me and being willing to speak with me, guide me, and comfort me. Even when I was a hardheaded, self-absorbed individual. I am thankful that I learned a relationship with Him was much more than religious practice and keeping rules or traditions. It is assurance, peace, and true life.

It is my hope that these stories, most about living the life of a firefighter, some about growing up, and some about just living life, will be a help to my brother and sister firefighters and anyone else who happens to read them.

Today I do not "toe the line" to try to be in right relationship with God. Today I give my heart to wanting to be obedient to my Lord because I am in right relationship with Him and I love Him. And He loves me and proves it daily in every breath I take.

All my life I have been told that I have an ability to tell a story well. I have also been told in Texas vernacular that I have some good "BS." I hope that now means "beneficial speech."

I want to thank everyone that encouraged me in putting these memories together. Family, brother and sister firefighters, some total strangers who have come across them on social media, my church, and of course the Holy Spirit who inspires me.

Having retired after thirty-five years from the fire service in November of 2020, I now act as a consultant to fire departments, lead the chapter of Central Texas Firefighters for Christ, and pastor a small church in a rural town.

CHAPTER 1

1

AROUND THE TABLE

AS I LOOK BACK ON SO MANY THINGS IN LIFE, which you tend to do when you get older, I find my memories often travel down a road that revisits times and events that left me with something valuable.

So many great experiences, lessons, wisdom and opportunities for laughter took place around "the table."

As a child, "the table" was the one the family would sit at. It doubled as a dinner table and a family meeting area when it was too cold to be on the porch. I listened to everything from Bible lessons to my parents' exploits while growing up on the farm. I heard hilarious stories and stories of hardships through WWII. I heard about life from parents born in 1919.

Having the bright idea of joining the Navy at age seventeen, I found there was a table in the gunner's workshop where we would share our home life stories, our struggles, and young men's dreams of the future.

Having a family of my own and sitting in the "Dad" position, I did the same as my parents as we sat around the table, sharing what I had learned and listening to what the kids were asking or experiencing as they anticipated the future or wrestled with the things in their young lives.

Becoming a firefighter, I found "the table" to again be an important part of the culture. Around it, I heard stories from the old lieutenants about big fires they had fought. I listened as brother firefighters poured out their hopes and fears after that run at 2 AM. We laughed, we hoped, we planned, we lived. Great memories.

I also remember that it was around a table that Jesus so often gathered those He loved. He listened to their hopes, their struggles and fears. He told them things to help them understand and He promised they had something ahead of them that would be wonderful. He showed them that struggles came and went, but He would always be the same. He took time to be present with them.

I am sure the table looked different than what we know. The old table from my childhood, the steel table aboard ship, the long wooden bench table of the fire station, they all looked different. But they all have memories of great experiences, lessons, wisdom, and opportunities for laughter. They still guide me and fill me with thankfulness.

I cannot return to the table of my childhood or the naval ship. When I visit my firefighters they still have "their table" and I am so glad they do. As Chief, it's not quite the same for me. They deserve their own table.

Life moves fast. I miss "my tables." My parents and many siblings are gone on ahead, and the kids are grown and have their own tables, as they should. My Navy boys are a memory. The shift work in the station is done.

I can't have those tables anymore. But I am always able to gather with Jesus at "His table." That hasn't changed. And He always seems to be available to share or listen.

Again, life moves as fast as we let it. I think I will go sit at that table with Him more often. I need the experiences, lessons, wisdom, and opportunities to laugh and have joy that I always find there.

I remember I always leave that table with something valuable. I would recommend a seat at His table to anyone. I hope you can find the time to sit awhile.

Psalm 23:5

You prepare a table before me in the presence of my enemies; You anoint my head with oil; My cup runs over.

Brother Mark McAdams

2

TALKING LIKE A RADIO

MY DAD HAD A WAY OF TELLING ME, OR ANYONE else he thought needed to hear it, that they were maybe talking too much. He would say, "You talk like a radio," meaning non-stop. He told me often that when a person talked, it should mean something. I have come to understand that our words should be worth something.

Our words can do great things, like encourage someone, share things we have learned that can be helpful, comforting, and even bring laughter and express love. Our words can do a lot of negative things as well. The thing is, we get a choice.

Lots of talking going on right now. Rightfully so I guess. A lot of the words I hear during this virus situation reflect people's fear, confusion, and sometimes anger. That's not surprising, given the circumstances. There is a lot of repetitive talking from people "talking like radios." Maybe this helps us cope with a new and frightening thing.

I was thinking about what has been coming out of my mouth lately as I try to ensure my firefighters are as safe as they can be in this situation. Lots of talking.

I have figured out that the most important words I have spoken have been the ones I have directed to God. The reason they are the most important is because these words brought me the best results. Not because of what I have said, but because of the reply, the direction I receive.

God does not seem to mind when I "talk like a radio."

He understands my fear, confusion and even anger.

I know that my words to Him never fall on deaf ears. Maybe I should do more talking to God in prayer.

Daniel 10:19 reports the message that God sent to Daniel after he had been calling out to God.

"O man greatly beloved, fear not! Peace be to you; be strong, yes, be strong!" So when he spoke to me I was strengthened, and said, "Let my lord speak, for you have strengthened me."

It's normal that we might have moments of being concerned, confused, and afraid through these days. It's okay to pour ourselves out to God. It's even better to listen. He has great things to tell us and they all mean something. As you are reading this, please understand how much God loves you.

So, in all our talking, maybe try to make sure it is showing love and encouragement. And maybe direct more of your talking to the one who gives us the most wonderful and helpful replies.

Proverbs 3:5-7

Trust in the LORD with all your heart;
And lean not on your own understanding.
In all your ways acknowledge Him and He
will direct your path.

Do not be wise in your own eyes; Fear the
Lord and depart from evil.

3

HELMETS

I HAVE BEEN THINKING ABOUT HELMETS. I HAVE four in my home office, and they hang there in the order in which I received them. One yellow, one orange, one red and one white. They represent thirty-five years of service and all of the lessons, memories, victories, and failures that came with them. The helmets are stained by the smoke of the many different types of fire they have been through, and the colors have been changed by what they have been exposed to. The colors, the stains, the scratches, and dents show a picture of things I have experienced. Some wonderful and exciting moments, like getting that quick knock down on a fire and saving a home. Some sad and hard moments, like when you just could not get that thing done well enough or quickly enough to save someone.

But for each helmet, I had the chance to grow, to gain something that would help me down the road if I chose to let it. My life is reflected in those stained and scratched old helmets. Our lives go through heat, scratches, and moments of glory and joy. Together they make us who we are from the challenges we experienced. As we go through the journey in the time given us, in a world where there is much fear and doubt, remember that we have been in the heat before, suffered the wounds, taken the glorious with the heartbreaking moments.

You will make it through. I'm glad my helmets aren't still shiny and unused. They are more useful to me and others in my life now, than before they were used.

James 1:2-4

My brethren, count it all joy when you fall into various trials, knowing that the testing of your faith produces patience. But let patience have its perfect work, that you may be perfect and complete, lacking nothing.

4

WATCH THE INTERSECTIONS

TRAINING SOMEONE TO DRIVE A FIRE DEPART- ment apparatus always begins with some very basic safety rules. Make sure everyone is buckled up and ready before you leave the station. Make sure all compartment doors are securely shut. Make sure the overhead door is all the way up before you move forward... and the list of these safety rules goes on and on.

One driving rule the company officer always reiterates is to come to a complete stop at intersections. Never blow through a stop sign or red light, and be sure to slow down a bit and look, even if you have a green light.

One officer told me, "We want to meet the other fire apparatus at the fire, not in an intersection along the way." What he meant by this was that I needed to watch out for other firefighting units that were responding. The last thing we wanted to do was miss one of them coming and pull out in front of them.

So as a result of these reminders, I would always be quick to stop and look for traffic at the intersections, even if we were running Code 3. This was very difficult for young firefighters, because we want to be "first in" at the fire.

On one call I had my route to the emergency planned out in my mind. We did not have GPS in those days, but instead memorized all the streets and hydrant locations. Along the way, I stopped at an intersection as I headed north at the same time a ladder company arrived at the intersection heading east. I yielded to them to go first and allowed the ladder company to go through ahead of me.

To my surprise, they went straight through the intersection heading east. I already had a route in my head to continue north through the intersection.

When the ladder company went the other way, it dawned on me that I was about to go the wrong direction.

By allowing time at the intersection, I was given the proper direction to get to where I needed to be. Had I not yielded I would have gone the wrong way.

There is also another very important kind of intersection. Life intersections. That's where

God has put someone in my life, maybe just for a moment, and our paths cross. They intersect.

If I think about it, those are the times, the opportunities when I have to give or receive something. Either way, those intersections are one way God speaks to me or uses me.

Through any given intersection I can help or grow if I decide to. Sometimes I don't even realize it, but find out later that I gave or received something valuable that made a difference in my life or someone else's.

In our society today, many demands are put upon us and we are often rushing to get to the next thing. I wonder how many blessings we miss. I wonder how many people we pass who need our help, because we blew through an intersection where God intended us to stop.

How many words from the mouths of our children do we miss because we are blasting through the intersection?

How many broken and lonely hearts do we rush past?

The problem is, in today's world we too often blow through the intersection because we are moving so fast. No time to stop and experience what God has put before us as an opportunity to learn, to serve, or to appreciate.

Maybe it would be good if I slowed down and looked for the intersections of life. Maybe a few words with someone I come across in the course of my day. Maybe a call to someone who comes to mind.

Perhaps I should ensure that I drive through my Lord's neighborhood daily and spend some time at an intersection with Him. I hear that we can come across Him anytime and anywhere.

Maybe slower can be good.

Brother Mark

Luke 10:30-34

Then Jesus answered and said: "A certain man went down from Jerusalem to Jericho, and fell among thieves, who stripped him of his clothing, wounded him, and departed, leaving him half dead. Now by chance a certain priest came down that road. And when he saw him, he passed by on the other side. Likewise a Levite, when he arrived at the place, came and looked, and passed by on the other side. But a certain Samaritan, as he journeyed, came where he was. And when he saw him, he had compassion. So he went to him and bandaged his wounds, pouring on oil and wine; and he set him on his own animal, brought him to an inn, and took care of him."

5

THE FIRST BREATH AFTER

AS A KID IN THE NAVY, WE WERE TRAINED IN using an "OBA" or oxygen breathing apparatus. They were pretty clumsy devices but were used during onboard ship firefighting. The greatest part of using them was the moment you took it off.

Upon entering the fire service, I was greatly impressed by the ease of using an SCBA or "self-contained breathing apparatus," compared with the old OBA onboard ship.

What I came to find out over time was that though this wonderful device called an SCBA enabled us to work at length in an otherwise untenable environment, and I was very comfortable using it, it was still a lot different from breathing as we normally do. It took discipline to effectively work hard while wearing it. I also remember how grateful I was that we had this wonderful piece of equipment.

I still wear an SCBA from time to time. Mostly to go in and check the work one of my crews have performed. Nothing like working through multiple bottles as I used to do, and the crews of my department still do.

But every time I do, I get the experience of stepping out into that "clean air," removing the regulator and face piece, and taking in that first breath of open air. No sound of a regulator or air flow in the mask.

Just that wonderful open air. It feels wonderful! It revitalizes! It says, "It is safe and okay just to breath."

That air in the SCBA cylinder is good. But that first breath after is marvelous.

My days are always full and busy. The expression I have heard many times is, "I am too busy to breathe."

While not literal in a physical sense, I believe it is accurate in a mental, and certainly a spiritual sense.

We work, we take care of the many demands placed on us by career, by family, by life. We are breathing and thinking our work and responsibilities. These are all good and necessary things and we are called to apply ourselves to doing them well.

I just wonder: Are we ever taking the time to step out of this pace, this routine, this "air space," and actually breathing in the air of strength, guidance, and rest that is available to us? Are we taking the time to stop and breathe in life?

I know that nowadays we try to cycle our firefighters out to rehab quicker than we used to. They get to take a break "off the air pack," as we used to say.

They breathe. They replenish themselves. Then, most firefighters are eager to "get back in" and continue the work to be done.

Maybe we need to stop what we are doing, if even for a short while each day, and breathe in that "clean air" mentally and spiritually. Seek a different thing that can revitalize, strengthen, and prepare us to go on with the things that life demands.

Take in that breath that restores. It isn't found watching TV or distracting ourselves in one of a thousand other things.

It is found in a quiet time with God. It is found in His Word.

God spoke about this breath we need from Him. A special type of air that is always available with Him.

Isaiah 42:5

Thus says God the LORD,
Who created the heavens and
stretched them out,
Who spread forth the earth and that which
comes from it,
Who gives breath to the people on it,
And spirit to those who walk on it;

This life and all its demands, responsibilities and the things we are required and often privileged to give ourselves to, move us through our days quickly. And we get a little short on air at times.

Maybe we need to take off the burden of the pack, drop the regulator and face piece of the day's work, and take in that "first breath after" of the Spirit.

Then... We will be better prepared to gear up and meet the next task He lays before us.

John 20:21-22

So Jesus said to them again, "Peace to you!
As the Father has sent Me, I also send you."
And when He had said this, He breathed

on them, and said to them, "Receive the Holy Spirit."

If you are getting winded and tired, I encourage you to stop, and take in that "first breath after" each day.

God bless and keep you.

Brother Mark

6

THE SMELL OF FIRES PAST

ONE NIGHT I ARRIVED AT THE SCENE OF A FIRE in a single-family residence that my department was working. My crews had gotten a knockdown of an attic fire when I arrived and I got to just walk around and tell them and the commander what a good job they had done, because they had.

Being older, it occurred to me that the smell of the fire was taking my mind back to over three decades of fires I had worked with some really good people. It was a pleasant memory in its own way as I thought about all the people I had the honor of working with. It became bittersweet after I went and spoke with the family. A couple with three young kids, looking at a house with the roof burned off. My crew had done a great job, but the fire was through the roof on their arrival. They had saved three rooms, but the home these people had known was gone.

Looking at this family's faces, I remembered so many faces in the past.

Like the smell of the smoke, their faces brought back many things. Fires, motor vehicle accidents, many medical calls, it did not matter, there were so many faces of families that came to my mind.

I remember when my oldest daughter was very young, I would come home and she would say, "Daddy, you were at a fire last night."

I would always say, "Hey, I took a shower," to which she would respond, "I can still smell it."

And sometimes so can we.

Sometimes we carry the pain of something on us. Like lingering smoke, we remember. It does not have to be the results of an emergency scene. Sometimes it is regret of something in our past. A bad decision, words spoken or words withheld, actions taken.... or not taken.

And the smell of the smoke just stays with us.

I look at my life with the good and the bad memories, good and bad choices, and they both have a way of rekindling in my heart and mind time to time. They sometimes bring pain, sorrow and regret.

These can often be brought to us much as the smell of the smoke brought my memories.

But as I look back on these and choose to lay them before Christ, whether they be pain, sorrow, or regret, I am reminded by Him of a very important fact.

That smoke has been washed away. The smell has been cleansed out.

When I choose to allow Jesus to take these memories, pain, or regret, He reminds me that I am His now.

In thinking of this, the scripture from Daniel came to mind.

Three young men had been sentenced to be burned alive for not choosing to follow something false. Upon being sentenced, they decided to trust God and accept His outcome. They did not argue or try to fix it. They just trusted.

In the end, they were delivered. In fact, when the three men were thrown into the flames, someone swore they could see four men walking among the flames unaffected by them.

And when they came out...

Daniel 3:27

And the satraps, administrators, gover-nors, and the king's counselors gathered together, and they saw these men on whose bodies the fire had no power; the hair of their head was not singed nor were their

garments affected, and the smell of fire was
not on them.

And the smell of the fire was not upon them.

When the world presses in on us, whether it is pain, sadness, or regret over the past, remember...

Trust and realize that God carries your pain and sorrow.

Isaiah 53:3-4

He was despised and rejected by men,
A Man of sorrows and acquainted with grief.
And we hid, as it were, our faces from Him;
He was despised, and we did not esteem Him.
Surely He has borne our griefs
And carried our sorrows;
Yet we esteemed Him stricken,
Smitten by God, and afflicted.

The smell of smoke has been removed. We are a new creation in Christ.

2 Corinthians 5:17

Therefore, if anyone is in Christ, he is a new creation; old things have passed away; behold, all things have become new.

Remember who you belong to.
The smells of fires past have a way of drifting away when we do.

Brother Mark

7

CHECKING MY ARMOR

HAVING BEEN IN THE FIRE SERVICE FOR OVER half of my life, I have definitely seen some changes.

I haven't liked all of them. Some of the changes I would like to see "changed back."

However, there have been a lot of good changes. I recently had to rewrite our PPE standard operating procedures to meet changes in the standards that guide us.

I thought back to the times when we paid much less attention to the care and condition of our turnouts, or bunker gear. Whatever the tradition of a department chooses to call them. There was no "ten year" gear life standard or cleaning standard over thirty years ago.

One of the good changes is that we now take a lot more time making sure this protection is right. After all, it is the line of protection between us and the heat. And that is, of course, critical. But the gear does more than keep us separated from the heat. It also allows us to function within the heat to battle the fire and/or make the rescue. It enables us to fulfill our duty.

I remember when the process of getting new bunker gear involved a person having to do two things.

1. Ask for a new set.
2. Convince the tight-fisted logistics manager that you needed them.

I also remember that I did not want to do either one of those.

I did not want them because I liked my dirty old bunker gear. And I no doubt felt that I looked "seasoned" in them. I preferred the melted tar on the shoulders and back of my coat and the frayed pant cuffs. I liked the soot-stained color. I certainly did not want new gear because that was what "rookies" wore. "Rookies" was the term we applied to the new guys before someone said we should call them "new hires."

I also did not want new bunker gear because I was really comfortable in my old gear. It was "broken in" and would slide back down over my turn out boots easily. I looked very good (I thought anyway) and I was very comfortable in that old gear.

So of course, with this attitude of pride and complacency, there came a time when I had to "reap what I had sown," as it were.

Being nozzle man one particular night, I was set to go in as soon as the two other firefighters forced the front door of a duplex. Just a standard working fire in a residential structure. As I waited with the nozzle, down on one knee, the living room window vented and the flames rolled out over us briefly. We repositioned a bit and soon made entry.

The funny thing was, I had this incredible pain in the back of my left shoulder. The longer we worked, the worse it seemed to get. Even during the firefight it was distracting me and kept my mind somewhat off what I was doing.

We got the knockdown and I soon came out to shed my gear and have a look.

I was not critically burned, but I had received enough heat on the back of my left shoulder to cause three small blisters. Looking at my coat, I realized the thermal layer had separated where the sleeve met the shoulder. Taking it on and off repeatedly had "created an opening" where the heat passed right though the shell and the moisture barrier to say "hello" to my shoulder.

Now that I am older, and responsible for more people, I am adamant about my firefighters having proper and well-maintained bunker gear.

I remind them that this protects them so they can successfully do their job. It enables them to work even when the heat is upon them.

As I look at the things I count on in life to protect me and others, I cannot help but examine the "armor of my faith." The thing I count on to enable me to function even when "the heat is on" during this event we call life.

I need to look at how well I am "checking my armor" when it comes to fighting the spiritual fires that confront me and those around me.

Ephesians chapter 6 tells us to "Put on the **full** armor of GOD" so we can "extinguish the fiery darts of the wicked one." It describes this armor and leaves no part of the warrior uncovered. It does not say, "Helmet optional" or "maybe consider," it says **full** armor.

I take that to mean that we should make sure the armor is in right condition and always ready to do battle. After all, who knows in this life when a "fiery dart" may fly at us? It is one of those "Not if, but when" situations.

God instructs us to be prepared, properly "armored up."

Why? So when the heat of life comes and the fiery darts are flying, we can "**stand**."

If I want to stand, that means not fall when life brings its challenges. I need to make sure not only that I have my armor, but that it is also in the proper condition.

After all, we are told that we will be attacked by a "roaring lion" at times. *(1 Peter 5:8)*

My armor is kept by the presence of His Word in my life, my confidence in His salvation in my life, the relationship of prayer and time hearing the proper guidance in my life.

I am afraid that when the fiery darts fly, many Christians find their armor has some chinks in it.

We will stand strong in the trial if we stand strong and prepare during times of peace.

And when the heat comes upon us, the church, we will be able to continue to do our duty in service to our Lord because we have this protection in good order. Perhaps we should not wait to pray, to study, or to seek God until after the fiery darts start flying. After all, when you ask for this protection, instead of a tight-fisted logistics manager, you have an all-giving God to prepare you for whatever you may face.

If I meet the challenge today, will my heart be prepared? Have I gotten too comfortable in my way of doing things and maybe too complacent in preparing for the spiritual fights that will no doubt come?

I should check my armor daily. And get it renewed often.

After all, I should be able to serve, even when the heat is upon me.

Like my Savior did.

2 Timothy 2:15

Be diligent to present yourself approved to God, a worker who does not need to be ashamed, rightly dividing the word of truth.

Keep your armor right, and stand. You will need to be at your best when the fires come.

God Bless

Brother Mark

Ephesians 6:10-17

Finally, my brethren, be strong in the Lord and in the power of His might. Put on the whole armor of God, that you may be able to stand against the wiles of the devil. For we do not wrestle against flesh and blood, but against principalities, against powers, against the rulers of the darkness of this age, against spiritual hosts of wickedness in the heavenly places. Therefore take up the whole armor of God, that you may be able to withstand in the evil day, and having done all, to stand. Stand therefore, having girded your waist with truth, having put on the breastplate of righteousness, and having shod your feet with the preparation of the gospel of peace; above all, taking the shield of faith with which you will be able to quench all the fiery darts of the wicked one. And take the helmet of salvation, and the sword of the Spirit, which is the word of God.

CHAPTER 2

8

SOMETHING MISSING

I HAVE SAID FOR A LONG TIME THAT THE BEST part of my firefighting career was absolutely those I worked with. I had the privilege of working on crews that had a spirit of brotherhood I cannot really describe. In the station, responding to a call, on the call, the trip back to the house, and sitting around rehashing the call around the table. Talking, laughing, learning and living the firefighting life as we went.

Together.

I remember getting to work and finding out one of them had reported off sick or had scheduled vacation I had forgotten about. There was always a bit of a feeling of "something missing."

Usually another firefighter would be assigned from another station to fill their place. Good people, but there was still a feeling of something missing.

That chair they usually sat in was empty and the shift would be okay, but not the same.

It was always good to come in to work and everyone was there in the place they should be. There was a feeling of confidence, knowing that everyone and everything was in its right place. When together, we felt we could face and deal with whatever we were challenged with when the tones went off and we responded. Together.

Sometimes in life I get the feeling that there is something missing, something out of order, an emptiness. Everything seems in order but there is an "empty seat" in my life. How many times have I been moving through life, accomplishing what I want, yet something feels off, feels empty?

I have learned that in my haste, my busyness, my pursuit of what I want and what I think I need, I have often forgotten about someone who is very important. And in my haste, I have failed to realize that their absence has produced an emptiness in me, a feeling that something is off, not as it should be.

And I realize that there is an empty chair, a missing presence.

I get so involved in this life and I fail to realize that I have given no place for my Savior in my days as they hurry past. And I feel it.

I can try to fill His seat with someone or something else, but there is still a feeling of something missing.

But when I call out, when I seek Him, He always shows up and completes my life. He restores my feeling of security and readiness to face the next thing in life.

When He is there in my life where He should be, it is complete.

Exodus 33:14

And he said, "My presence will go with you, and I will give you rest."

Psalm 27:8

When you said, "Seek my face." My heart said to you, "Your face, Lord, I will seek."

May we have everyone, especially our Lord, in the right place in our lives as we face what is before is. If something feels like it is missing, call out to Him. The completeness He brings will show itself in our hearts and lives.

Brother Mark

9

IF I CAN SEE JUST
A GLIMMER...

AFTER MONTHS OF TRAINING IN THE FIRE academy, I remember making that first smoke-charged structure fire on the first in hose line and thinking, "You really can't see anything in here!"

I had been told this. We had experienced some live fire training, but it was different. Nothing. I could see nothing for the smoke. I was crawling behind a driver that was working up as lieutenant that shift and I had my doubts that we really had any idea where we were going. I knew I didn't.

I was surprised when he opened the nozzle, and I then saw flames kicking up from where he directed it. Then I heard him mumble "more hose" through his face piece and he started moving again. Following behind him, dragging hose, I found we were at the main body of the fire. We got a knockdown on the fire and at that point I felt like the Great American Firefighter. The fact was, all I had done was drag hose.

Back at the station later, we were doing what all firefighters do. We sat around and put the fire out several more times as we recounted the event.

I remember this driver saying, "I finally saw the glow and got to the seat of the fire."

In future interior fire situations, I made myself slow down and simply observe the conditions. And as he had said, in the midst of the rolling smoke and darkness, for a brief second, you might see the glimmer of the flame. This would give you a direction to move in to find the body of the fire in the zero visibility conditions. The smoke would be distracting, but if you looked and found that glimmer, you could get reoriented and make progress. Even in the darkness.

Life moves quickly, and there are so many distractions. Things get really dark in this world sometimes. And it gets difficult to see which direction we need to go, what decision is best, or what action we should or should not take. We have to make decisions on and in life for not only ourselves, but often try to do the right thing for those we care about.

When I face these times, I know I will make it through if I can only stop, be patient for a moment, and find the light I need to direct me. If I can only get a glimmer, I can move forward. That glimmer is the direction the light of the Holy Spirit gives if I will only stop and look for it.

As I pray, and as I get myself out of the way and trust that the light is going to show itself, it always happens that the light will shine and give me direction. And in that direction, I can have peace, knowing I am not only moving forward, but moving forward in the right direction. In that direction I come upon assurance, hope, and strength.

Life gets difficult, confusion is often at hand, but the light of Jesus' promises never fail to show themselves.

If we can only take time to get a glimmer of His light, it will lead us to the full light of His love for us and the glorious purpose He has for each of us.

Keep your eyes open for the glimmer..

Brother Mark

2 Corinthians 4:6

For it is the God who commanded light to shine out of darkness, who has shone in our hearts to give the light of the knowledge of the glory of God in the face of Jesus Christ.

10

BOOSTER TANK

IT SEEMS IN THE FIRE SERVICE THAT WE PAY A lot of attention to tanks of different types and how much is contained in them.

My first lieutenant used to say "air tank" when referring to his self-contained breathing apparatus cylinder. We have O2 tanks, and of course fuel tanks.

We have guidelines that tell us that they should be kept in a ready state of being full.

Minimum of 4000 PSI on the air cylinder, 1000 on the O2. No less than three-quarters tank of fuel on the apparatus. We do this to be ready to respond.

But then there is the booster tank, water carried onboard the apparatus.

No partial tank allowed. Always kept at full capacity. Having a low booster tank for any reason other than actively fighting fire is unacceptable.

The booster is for an initial attack. It is not intended to always be enough water for a substantial working fire. It is for small events or sometimes to get "started with" until a sustained water source, a hydrant supply, is established.

Even after a supply is established, the pump operator is taught to refill the tank to capacity as soon as possible in case the hydrant supply fails. Then the inside crew has something to protect them if this occurs.

I was thinking about my "spiritual tank." It's what I carry with me to live out faith, to face "the events" that I face in life.

It occurred to me that this is another tank that I should always ensure is at full capacity.

I keep it full by frequently going to my sustained source of supply. I need to ensure that I am staying full by taking in the Word of God, by spending time in His presence, and by fellowship with other believers.

Unfortunately, I sometimes let my spiritual tank get low. When I face the big events that life inevitably presents, the challenges that take everything I have, I find myself running dry and I get overrun.

The last thing I ever want to hear on the fire ground is one of my operators coming on the radio and saying, "Out of water."

The last thing I should do is run with a low tank spiritually.

The good news is that we have a "reliable source" for that sustained supply. I don't have to enter the spiritual fights that life presents with my own limited resources. I get to hook into that "strong hydrant" of the Word, the Holy Spirit and trust.

I need to always keep my heart "topped off" in the truth gained in my prayer life. I need to check this tank regularly.

When the world and its demands have me so busy, with so many demands on my time and life, it is sometimes easy to procrastinate in topping off the tank of our faith.

Scripture reminds us that we need to give this attention.

Romans 15:13

Now may the God of hope fill you with all joy and peace in believing, that you may abound in hope by the power of the Holy Spirit.

Keep your booster tank full by hooking to the hydrant regularly.

You will need the sustained supply when life's events present themselves.

We cannot fight on our own limited supply.

Brother Mark

11

BE QUIET AND COUNT

AS I NOW SIT AND THINK OF ALL OF THE TIME I spend keeping up with all of the information that comes to me, and trying to keep up with all the changes that affected our fire department and our people, I realize that life is filled with many responsibilities, trials and decisions to be made. Lots of info being sent to everyone to do this and not do that. All well-intentioned, I think.

I at one point in my life had to make a decision about the many things we have to face as we journey through this life. Things that bring fear or worry to the forefront. The unexpected challenges we face on a daily basis where we must make decisions. Often these are decisions that impact others besides ourselves.

I decided that if I take time to gather all the facts, things will make better sense. I decided that I should stop, be quiet, and count up not only the current challenges, but also the things that are good and right in my life, in my day-to-day existence. In counting, I always find that there is more to be grateful for than things to worry uselessly over. And from the counting I get a result, a sum, of peace. The blessings and good generally outweigh the difficulties. In practicing this, I get the peace and the strength to move forward to the next right thing I have to do.

Take time to be quiet, and count.

Brother Mark

Philippians 4:8-9

Finally, brethren, whatever things are true, whatever things are noble, whatever things are just, whatever things are pure, whatever things are lovely, whatever things are of a good report, if there is anything praiseworthy-meditate on these things. The things which you learned and received and heard and saw in me, these do, and the God of peace will be with you.

12

FROM A DEAD SLEEP

ONE INESCAPABLE PART OF A CAREER IN FIRE-
fighting is being brought out of a sound sleep, sometimes several times each night, by a very loud noise, then the lights kicking on, and immediately jumping on a truck that makes very loud noises while you are listening to a dispatcher inform you as to the reason for this rude awakening and rapid departure from a warm bed. It just comes with the job.

The loud tone that emits from a speaker in the ceiling and the lights coming on while the dispatcher or a computer-generated voice calls out the name of your unit and politely requests that you respond to a certain address for a certain type of emergency are all intended to bring a firefighter out of a dead sleep.

Even with all of this wonderful assistance, a firefighter sometimes fails to wake up. The hardline officers in those days would leave firefighters if they weren't on the truck. But usually someone would run back to shake them out of dreamland. I found that every once in a while, a firefighter would make it to the truck and still be somewhat asleep.

I recall noticing that one fellow did not show up at the truck on about our third call of the night. He had gotten out of bed but was walking in circles behind the truck while holding a pillow. Truth was, he was moving about but was still very much asleep.

The fact is, we could not get the job done if we remained asleep. If we wanted to serve the public, we had to wake up and pay attention to what we needed to do. After all, it was a very serious job and what we did was very important to those who called on us.

As a follower of Christ, I know that we (that is, the church, and by that I mean the people, not a denomination or organization) have a very important calling. That calling is to love our Lord above all else and show the love of Christ to the world around us.

But I see that we the church can sometimes fall into a dead sleep, and in so doing fail to respond when called upon.

We get really tired dealing with life sometimes. Life distracts us and can wear us down. We feel like we don't have anything left, or get so wrapped up in ourselves we fail to hear the call of God.

Maybe we attend some church gatherings and we say, "Well, I did my part."

Truth is, we are just walking in circles, holding our pillows. Doing our religious thing but never waking up to the glory of God around us. Never knowing the fullness of living out God's purpose in our lives. We just hug our pillows and stay asleep.

I believe we live in a time when God is calling us, His church, to action.

But we won't fulfill it unless we all individually wake up and decide that what we are called to is important. Eternally important.

It is a time when the church needs to rise up out of its dead sleep and experience the power of God's love in us. With it, we can bring that love to a world that needs it. Our purpose.

Religious practice won't bring us out of this sleep. Only our willingness to turn our hearts fully to His call will accomplish that. After all, what He calls us to is important.

Let us wake up and hear the directions from our Lord.

Let's be sure we don't miss a call.

Ephesians 5:14-16

Therefore He says: "Awake, you who sleep, Arise from the dead, And Christ will give you light." See then that you walk circumspectly, not as fools but as wise, Redeeming the time, because the days are evil.

Brother Mark

13

A SEAT FOR A STRANGER

I HAD THE PLEASURE OF BEING A KID WHO GREW
up in "small town" America.

I lived on Main Street, exactly four blocks from
the downtown district. The downtown district consisted of two blocks of a variety of stores on each
side of the street. We had "frontier days" in July,
with a parade, street dance, and a carnival, to name
a few of the activities.

Before being old enough to go work on my
dad's roofing crew, summer was for floating on
the creek that flowed through the center of town,
playing baseball, and building forts... at least *after*
doing the chores Dad had left for me.

We had one police officer who went home at 6
PM unless someone called him, and they rarely did.

It was a wonderful and safe place to grow up.

Another thing that ran through our town was the
railroad. The tracks ran east/west about 300 yards

north of Main Street. This was also a place of childhood activity, such as seeing who could walk a rail the longest without falling off. Or chunking rocks at the train as it went by if no adults were in view.

Dad always warned us about the "Hobos" riding the rails. He worked the railroad for a while and was familiar with these mysterious fellows. He would tell Mom to keep the "door latched" when she was home alone, because you never knew who might wander off those tracks.

One of the few things one might actually be concerned about in that little town.

Main Street, the creek, the railroad tracks ... our town.

In our town on Sunday afternoons, following the required big "Sunday dinner," (because we did not say lunch in the South back then, dinner was the middle of the day and supper was in the evening), weather permitting my dad, older brothers and visiting family would gather under the big pecan tree in lawn chairs, drink iced tea, and talk about thousands of things while the younger boys played ball in the big yard or some other activity.

The ladies stayed inside and visited. Male children were forbidden from entering the house on a Sunday afternoon. My Dad would say, "The weather is too nice to be inside." He would allow us on the porch if there was a lightning or hailstorm. This did not apply to the girls. They did whatever they wanted.

In the summer of 1969 was one of those typical Sundays.

Church gathering had been attended and a large meal had been consumed. Dad and other men of the family had gathered under the pecan tree for relaxing and talking. I was about the same age as my oldest brother's sons, so we were playing an intense game of hide-and-seek around the house, as I recall.

Coming down the street leading from the tracks came a man who in those days we described as a hobo. A person who jumped the rail cars and moved about like a gypsy.

To my great surprise, this hobo fellow walked across Main Street, and came into our yard and approached the group of men clustered under the pecan tree.

I called out to my nephews to "Come watch this." I assumed Dad would put him on the road right away. I had seen several hobos, but they always had stayed down around the tracks.

We kids, of course, eased our way closer to see what was going to happen.

Sure enough, my dad stood up and took several steps toward this man who came off the rails. The man was a bit older, a little dirty and was wearing several day's growth of beard.

I immediately felt a bit of sorrow for the old guy and wondered how this was going to turn out, given the warnings I had heard Dad give Mom about these fellows.

I heard my dad say to the man, "How are doing today? What can I do for you?"

I was a bit relieved by this because as I said, I felt a little sorry for the old fellow and really thought Dad would react poorly to this bold approach by him on a Sunday afternoon.

The hobo replied, "Sir, I was hoping maybe you had some work I could do for you to get a bite to eat. I have not eaten in quite a while and I am really hungry."

My dad reached out and grabbed the old fellow by the arm, just above the elbow. I initially thought he was going to usher him back to the rails. Dad had a reputation for having a hot temper and willingness to resort to fisticuffs if he thought it was needed.

I was not aware of it then, but I saw obedience to something the Bible tells us lived out that day. My dad did not send the hobo on his way. He did something that has touched me and been an example for me all of my life.

Instead, he led the man to his *own* lawn chair. A chair that none of us dared sit in because he had made it *abundantly clear* that this chair was *not for general use.* It was *his* lawn chair.

He sat the man down and said, "You wait right here."

Dad then strode to the back door of the house, and upon entering the screened-in back porch, I heard him calling, "Momma, come here a minute."

There was soon bustling about the kitchen, while my dad dashed out with a "TV table" as we called it. A small folding table made to accommodate one person so they could eat and watch television. He parked the TV table in front this man and said, "Do you like iced tea?"

The man said, "Yes sir," looking a little confused at this point.

Off my Dad went again and returned with iced tea. Then he was back to the house and came out with two fully loaded plates of Momma's homemade enchiladas, rice, pinto beans, salad, and coconut cake, which he placed before the man.

The man teared up, and he said, "I will work for this."

My dad, who *very often* said, "If you want to eat you better want to work in this life," replied, *"I have been hungry before myself, and I am blessed with too much food in this house to let a man go hungry."* Then he sat and talked to the man as he was eating. I think he just did not want the man to feel awkward.

After a while the man laid down his fork, looked at my dad with a sorrowful expression on his face, and said, "I am so sorry, sir, but I cannot eat all of this food!"

I suppose he felt like he would insult my dad if he could not eat it all.

Dad replied, "That's all right, my friend, we will wrap it up to take with you. You might get hungry *again later* or run into *someone you can share it with that needs it."*

My dad prepared the food in a paper bag, handed it to the man, and then said, "Do you need to stay and rest a while?"

I believe that man would in the very least have gotten a rollaway bed on the porch of our little house if he had wanted it.

The man was at a loss for words, and then the train whistle blew. He looked toward the tracks, looked back at my dad, and said "I have to go, sir. You have given a man like me all I need."

And he walked away.

That day, my dad taught me something valuable.

He taught me that love of others is the essential thing, no matter how different they may be.

He taught me to give something to others that would be valuable to them later and perhaps bless someone else down the line.

1 John 3:16-18

By this we know love, because He laid down His life for us. And we also ought to lay down our lives for the brethren. But whoever has this world's goods, and sees his brother in need, and shuts up his heart from him, how does the love of God abide in him? My little children, let us not love in word or in tongue, but in deed, and in truth.

Always have a seat for the stranger.

Brother Mark

14

THE VISITOR

IN MY WORK, I GET A LOT OF VISITORS. A LOT of people put their head in my office door and want to talk. Some need to talk business. After all, I am at work.

A lot of young people work for me and they often want to talk about something on their mind, or just listen to this old man ramble. I am sure I give them a laugh or two, even if I don't mean to. I welcome this, as I am glad they trust me as someone to talk with.

I got a visitor today. I did not even notice him at first and he just stood to the side of the room, not saying much. Then I got a phone call regarding a business situation that was a bit of a problem.

I heard my visitor mumble something. I made the mistake of asking, "What did you say?"

The visitor said, "That's a big problem I heard you talking about. It probably will turn out really bad, you should be worried."

I had not thought of it that way, but I began to think that maybe this was going to go bad in a big way. I started feeling a bit worried.

My visitor then said, "Those people that caused this problem are deliberately trying to make things harder for you."

I had not thought of that either, and I now started getting a little mad and resentful.

"No telling where this may turn out for you," said my visitor. "You may get a lot of backlash from your directors about this, and your employees are probably criticizing you right now."

Well now I was worried and mad, and at this point I begin to get a little fearful. "What is going to come of this?" I wondered. I was confused, because a few minutes ago it was just dealing with the regular issues of a day's business, just life. Now I was thinking about this, and it seemed really big and bad.

It was at that point I realized who my visitor was.

I also realized I had received visits from him before.

I remembered that he was a known liar who was always going around, trying his best to change something small into major ordeals. He was very good at steering people down the roads of fear and anger.

I remembered also that just this morning I had spoken with a close friend who had told me everything was going to work out and He would always be by my side when I needed Him. He is a great friend I have known for quite a while, and lately we have begun growing very close. He has always kept His word to me. He has never broken His word even once.

It occurred to me that whenever this great friend of mine and I started growing close, I would get more visits from this visitor who lingered in the corner. Yes, I remembered him.

I decided that I did not need or want to spend any more time with this visitor.

I remembered that I did not have to.

So I called my dear friend and told Him the things this visitor was telling me. My friend assured me these things I was being told were not true.

My friend said, "Why don't you just let me in your office a minute?"

Funny thing. When my friend showed up, there just was not any room for that visitor anymore.

After that, I had the most wonderful day after I spoke with my dear friend for a while. I realized that I never needed to let that particular visitor remain in my office. Let alone pay attention to him.

Before He left, my greatest friend told me, "Let me know if that particular visitor shows up again. After all, he is a known thief."

Jesus warns us about this one who visits to steal, kill, and destroy.

He often comes when we are doing well to steal our peace, kill our hope, and destroy our faith.

Remember, this visitor can only do this if we let him hang around and listen to him. We have a choice who we keep company with and listen to.

Y'all watch the company you keep. God bless.

Brother Mark

Mark

"And these are the ones by the wayside where the word is sown. When they hear, Satan comes immediately and takes away the word that was sown in their hearts."

1 Peter

Likewise you younger people, submit your-selves to your elders. Yes, all of you be submissive to one another, and be clothed with humility, for "God resists the proud, but gives grace to the humble." Therefore humble yourselves under the mighty hand of God, that He may exalt you in due time, casting all your care upon Him, for He cares for you. Be sober, be vigilant; because your adversary the devil walks about like a roaring lion, seeking whom he may devour. Resist him, steadfast in the faith, knowing that the same sufferings are experienced by your brotherhood in the world.

CHAPTER 3

15

TAILBOARD REVIEW

ONE OF THE THINGS I ALWAYS FOUND INTER-
esting was that after a working fire, after the mop
up and the roll up, we would all meet at the tailboard of the first in engine and have a review of the
actions taken during the fire.

A critique, as it were.

But in addition to the review, we would essen-
tially "put the fire out" again. We would recount the
actions we took and tell how we advanced the line,
forced the door, found the seat of the fire, and did
the primary search, and anything else that would
add to the adventure.

I realized after a while that we were "putting
the fire out again" in more ways than one.

We would learn from one another as we con-
ducted this "tailboard review." We also worked
through and processed the hard parts of the event
as we shared.

And inevitably, by the time we got back to the station, this conversation would expand into previous fires worked and lessons learned in the past. We would recount the rights and the wrongs of our decisions on the scene of previous fires. We learned things from the more experienced that we could use in the future.

From the experience gained at that day's fire and the knowledge shared, we gained in confidence to better meet and deal with the next one.

I have found that when I go through difficult times in life, I have the chance to be confident because of things I have already experienced and the wisdom shared with me by those I respect.

I also realize that I have the opportunity to be confident in Christ. Within my relationship with Christ, I can count on His wisdom and also remember what He has done every time I have called on Him.

In this "review," I can gain strength to meet the next challenge in life.

In this "review," I can be confident in remembering what God has done before.

When the Children of Israel would face a trial, God would remind them who they were and who they belonged to. He would also remind them of what He had already done.

Deuteronomy 8:2

And you shall remember that the LORD your God led you all the way these forty years in the wilderness, to humble you [and] test you, to know what [was] in your heart, whether you would keep His commandments or not.

The next time the trials of life present themselves to us, maybe we should conduct a review, remember what He has done before in our lives, review the wisdom shared with us by Him, and walk forward in faith.

What we have been through will strengthen us in what we yet have to go through.

We will see that what He has shown us in the past has a purpose in the now.

God bless. Stay strong in Him.

Brother Mark

16

THE SOUNDS BEFORE THE FALL

AS A FIRE CADET THIRTY-FIVE YEARS AGO, ONE of the topics of study the instructors gave a lot of attention to was building construction. Having had some experience in this subject, I can remember how interesting it was to hear the instructors point out how fire had its effect on a structure, depending on how it was put together and the components used to build it.

Back then, they would sometimes drag out some old reel films that addressed the subject. I remember one of the films that talked about signs and sounds of imminent structure collapse that the firefighter should look out for. The narrator had a very deep voice and repeated the instruction to "listen for the groaning" of the building, which was an indication the building was shifting, its structural members were compromised, and it could no longer bear its own weight.

The advice of the narrator was always to look, listen, and remain aware of what was going on with the structure.

Over time, I know that all firefighters at some point have the experience of listening to the death of a structure. The main thing that must be adhered to is to get out of the place of danger before a collapse occurs. If the fire is controlled before enough damage occurs, the structure can sometimes be saved.

I was reading where some estimates indicate that 85 percent of mainstream churches in America are in decline, or have plateaued when it comes to those who take part in serving and worshipping with a local church body, as well as those coming to faith in Christ. I realize the church is actually the followers of Christ and not a building, a certain denomination or organization.

Some studies estimate the rate of local church bodies completely disbanding is around 1,000 per month in our country. I cannot help but wonder if we have failed to see that the "building is being compromised." That there have been groaning's for a long time that we have not paid attention to.

Perhaps we have allowed some crucial elements of our structure to be removed or improperly altered, increasing the likelihood of a collapse.

Maybe we just have not been watching and listening. It did not happen overnight.

A fire crew's enemy is complacency. Getting comfortable in the "way we do things," our traditions, makes us less likely to hear, or even seek God's guidance.

This applies to the church body, but the church body is made up of each individual follower of Christ.

Maybe we should stop and look at how the foundation of the church, individually and as a body of believers, is put together.

Maybe we had better look and ensure that its components are built with the truth, power, and love of our Savior.

Now, more than ever, the world needs the church to stand strong and share the good news of the Gospel, to fulfill the Great Commission given us.

If we build it on Jesus, we will not fail. If we have built on religious traditions or what we want it to be, or how we feel comfortable, it cannot help but fail.

We need to "listen for the groaning," and ask God to show us how to save this house, and within that, fulfill His Great Commission.

Matthew 7:24-27

"Therefore whoever hears these sayings of Mine, and does them, I will liken him to a wise man who built his house on the rock; and the rain descended, the floods came, and the winds blew and beat on that house; and it did not fall, for it was founded on the rock. But everyone who hears these sayings of Mine, and does not do them, will be like a foolish man who built his house on the sand: and the rain descended, the floods came, and the winds blew and beat on that house; and it fell. And great was its fall."

Matthew 16:18

"And I also say to you that you are Peter, and on this rock I will build My church, and the gates of Hades shall not prevail against it."

Let us be the true church.

Brother Mark

17

ONE MISSING GLOVE...

"Check your turnouts every shift." This is pounded into every cadet at every firefighter academy. I recall one instructor saying, "As sure as you don't check your gear, you will be missing a glove."

I FOUND THIS TO BE TRUE OVER THE YEARS.

You get back to the station after a working fire and one glove is mysteriously missing. I never remember losing both, always just one. I guess gloves and socks are the same in that way.

The thing about the firefighter's glove is that you simply cannot function with one glove. You might pull that off with other types of gloves, but not a firefighter glove. That one exposed hand in the heat of the fire would quickly prevent you from staying in the place you needed to be to get the job done.

I remember two occasions in which a hose team was ready to make entry and one of them could not find one glove. That firefighter missing a glove had to step back and someone else had to take their place to go in and knock the fire down, do the search, get the job done.

In firefighting, you have to have everything in place and quickly accessible. It doesn't matter if everything else is there. Helmet, boots, hood, coat, pants, suspenders, air pack, mask and even one glove can be in place. But if *one* thing is left out, you cannot do the job.

As I face life each day, I find that the same holds true. Alarm clock set, clothes prepared for the day, list of things that must be done, are all in order. But when I leave out the protection and guidance from God by failing to spend time with Him in prayer, I enter the day missing something extremely vital.

And during that day, when I feel the heat of life's demands, I find myself struggling to meet them. I am missing the peace that I only get from His hand on me. I may have everything else in place. But the absence of that peace often prevents me from being where I should be: in His peace, under His guidance and moving forward by His strength.

1 Peter 5:6-7

Therefore humble yourselves under the mighty hand of God, that He may exalt you in due time, casting all your care upon Him, for He cares for you.

Keep yourself covered and your hand available for God to use.

Brother Mark

18

PULLING THE CEILING...

BEFORE I HAD ANY IDEA WHAT EXTINGUISHING a structure fire entailed, I had the notion that you simply pulled a hose inside, found the fire, sprayed water, done.

Of course, I soon found out that you often were required to dig into the structure to find the main body of the fire.

I wish I had a dollar for every time I heard the order, "Pull the ceiling, check the attic." Fire by nature makes its way up, and once it enters the open area of the attic, it grows and spreads quickly.

Once the fire was knocked down in a room there was always the real possibility that it had extended up into the attic, and unknown to you, could be burning aggressively over your head. The ceiling restricted your view and access and had to be removed.

Using tools called "pull down hooks," or any other tool you had at hand, you had to pull the

Sheetrock or other ceiling material down so you could get a view of the fire working powerfully over your head and make access to it. Once this was done, you could see the fire and understand what it was doing. Then you had the ability to determine what action to take.

Ceilings were just in the way.

In the last year, I have recognized other types of ceilings in my life. And they also have had to be removed.

Fear and anger are presented to me from multiple formats. Sometimes from a friend or even family member who fears societal conditions, changes in politics and government. Sometimes from news and social media. Fear about health and finances. Fear of tomorrow and what it might bring.

What I see is that this fear creates a ceiling. And it needs to be removed.

This "ceiling of fear" prevents us from seeing a powerful working force over us.

The Bible tells us over 300 times to not be afraid. It must be important. The scripture says things like "fear not," don't be afraid," "be anxious over nothing," and "don't let your heart be troubled."

Fear becomes a ceiling that prevents us from seeing and accessing the powerful working of God.

Fear is a ceiling that takes away our view of truth, compassion for others, and the love God bestows upon us.

Fear is a ceiling that blocks the view of God's presence in our lives.

Fear shows us a false view.

Fear is the basis of anger, doubt, worry, resentment, remorse and even hatred. And fear's end result is hopelessness.

This ceiling needs to be removed to give us access to the power and strength and love of God. It is difficult for fear and faith to reside together. One will always be stronger than the other.

When the uncertainty of the world becomes a ceiling between me and God, I remember what God did so that we could gain access to His presence and know His love, strength, and comfort. He gave of Himself on the cross, and it is said the curtain that divided the people from the holy altar was torn in two.

Now the ceiling was pulled and the full view and presence of God in everyone's life could be known if they chose it.

God reminds us that His place of power and authority has not diminished and He can be trusted.

I encourage everyone to pull the ceiling of fear in today's world, behold the fire of God's presence, and obtain the view that can then direct us on the paths of our lives.

Remember that there is a powerful force working over us.

Pull the ceilings that are hindering your view of what God is doing. Look up.

Psalm 5:2-3

Give heed to the voice of my cry,
My King and my God,
For to You I will pray.
My voice you shall hear in the
morning, O LORD;
In the morning I will direct it to you,
And I will look up.

Isaiah 51:6

Lift up your eyes to the heavens,
And look on the earth beneath.
For the heavens will vanish away like smoke,
The earth will grow old like a garment,
And those who dwell in it will die in
like manner;
But My salvation will be forever,
And My righteousness will not be abolished.

Brother Mark

19

MOVE UP...

A FEW TIMES IN EVERYONE'S FIREFIGHTING career, they will experience a once-in-a-lifetime type of situation.

Some of mine have been a tornado that took twenty-seven lives, a chlorine tanker leak, and a large chemical fire, to name a few. These are the type of calls we may not experience but once or twice in a career.

As I sat in my office during the initial weeks of the COVID 19 pandemic, I became aware of the fact that at least 75 percent of my energy and time was being directed toward issues stemming from this pandemic: changing response protocols, tracking PPE, conference calls and on and on.

In a way it seemed like everything else was kind of standing still.

We didn't know what was next as we were facing something new. All we could do was be available and ready to face the next thing presented us.

I kept thinking about the "move ups" that we would do when a big fire was going on.

The purpose of the move up was to get people in places that were short of coverage. As the number of alarms increased for a working fire, first, second, third alarms, the closer a unit was "moved up" toward the fire.

I feel like the church is being called to "move up," and prepare to go to work for the kingdom.

I remember that the closer we got moved to the incident, the more we would monitor the radio, hoping we would hear something that would tell us they were about to bust another alarm and we could make the fire. You see, we really wanted to make the fire, go to work, and have the experience of being in the fight.

I hope that I can be as excited about God moving me closer to service each day. I hope my drive to want to go to work for Him is as important as it was in the job.

I also remember that every time we were moved up, got a little closer to the fire, we made sure we had everything in order for when we finally responded to the scene. Gloves? One right, one left, in appropriate pockets. Hood? Yep. Air cylinder full and ready? Absolutely.

I believe that God is moving His church closer to a mighty work.

I hope you are listening closely to Him.

I hope you are taking this time to make sure you are ready.

I hope you are anxious to go to work for His kingdom.

I hope you can see that every day we are moved into a position to provide coverage. Every day you can be used right where you are, and there are bigger works to come.

It may be quiet right now. Your attention may be getting focused on the things at hand.

Remember, His church may be moved up, called up, in any moment.

Stay safe and God bless.

Brother Mark

2 Timothy 4:2

Preach the word! Be ready in season and out of season. Convince, rebuke, exhort, with all longsuffering and teaching.

20

KEEP PUSHING, KEEP LEARNING, KEEP GROWING... THERE IS NO ROOM FOR QUIT...

AS A DRIVER ASSIGNED TO AN ENGINE COMPANY, I had the privilege of working for yet another great lieutenant. One of the pieces of advice he gave me was, "Keep pushing to stay in shape, keep learning and you will always keep growing toward being a better firefighter, because there is no room for quit in what we do."

He did his part by making sure we worked out, trained every shift, and kept our minds on the fact that often when people called for our help, we were the last chance they had.

The fire service has changed in many ways over the years. One of those ways has been in the new and improved tools we have had to work with over the years. My lieutenant would say, "That's a good tool if you learn how to use it. Otherwise it just takes up room on the truck."

There was a lot to learn. A lot to remember. But he taught us it was important to keep growing as firefighters by training, by taking care of ourselves, our apparatus, our equipment, and especially one another. In that way we could take care of those who called for our help. That was our duty.

We put much time and effort into this growth because he taught us its importance. We believed in it. And many times, we saw that work pay off in performing our job.

I have been thinking about the other things in my life I believe in, that I think are important and I am called to do.

My faith, my relationship with God, and my service to Him.

Am I expected to grow, learn, and get stronger?

I owed my very best to those who called upon me in my work.

Do I have the passion for Jesus who gave everything for me as I did for my career?

Is what my lieutenant taught us about our job just as applicable to my life with God?

I think it was a great lesson God gave me in that lieutenant's wisdom.

I have the privilege of knowing God better and of being closer to Him and hearing His guidance in my life. My realization of His presence grows each day, and it is worth it to keep pushing when life is difficult, to keep learning of Him and His purpose for me, so I can grow stronger in peace as I grow closer to Him.

Christ never quit on His Journey to the cross.

There was no room for quit because we are important to Him.

Let us keep seeking and growing in His love, strength, and peace. It is worth it.

1 Corinthians 15:58

Therefore, my beloved brethren, be steadfast, immovable, always abounding in the work of the Lord, knowing that your labor is not in vain in the Lord.

Brother Mark

21

CLEANING HOUSE

IT IS THAT TIME OF YEAR. SPRING HAS ARRIVED and now it is time to clean up what winter left behind. The yard is trimmed of dead branches, and those leaves from fall we kept ignoring are gathered up. When I was a child, we would have the spring cleaning of the house. This was a much-dreaded day, as Momma shifted into a mode of military officer and ordered the removal of all rugs and mattresses from the house and into the sunlight to receive "a good beating," as she called it. Screens were removed and hosed down, windows were washed, items that had lost their usefulness were discarded, and even the siding on the house got a good scrubbing.

As a child I found this day to be quite painful and I had multiple failed escape attempts from this unpleasant endeavor.

But I had to confess even then that when we had finished with the hard work of cleaning and purging the house, it just felt good.

We celebratee the triumphal entry of Jesus into Jerusalem on Palm Sunday, when He began His journey to the cross to die on our behalf and overcome death by His resurrection.

In between His triumphal entry and the cross, Jesus was not idle.

After weeping over what was to come of the city of Jerusalem and what was to become of these people He loved, Jesus cleaned house. Observing that the Temple, which had been built to be a place of prayer, service to, and communion with God, had been turned into a place of corruption that took advantage of those who had come to worship, Jesus decided that some cleaning up was in order.

Jesus Cleanses the Temple

Luke 19: 45-48

Then He went into the temple and began to drive out those who bought and sold in it, Saying to them, "It is written, 'My house is a house of prayer, but you have made it a 'den of thieves.' And He was teaching daily in the temple. But the chief priests, the scribes, and the leaders of the people sought to destroy Him, And were unable to do anything; for all the people were very attentive to hear Him.

After getting things cleaned up, Jesus, knowing that His hour was soon coming and He would be crucified, went about what He needed to do. He continued to teach the people, knowing that His appointed hour at the cross was soon coming.

We should take this time to reflect on what things are in our lives we perhaps no longer have a use for, and clean them out. As we Christians look at this time in which we observe the merciful gift of the cross and the glorious resurrection of our Lord Jesus, may we seek from Him direction on what things in our lives are coming between us and the joy of knowing Him as our Savior.

It is easy to get distracted by this world and the things in it. There are many demands put upon all of us as well. I pray we put aside all things that we may have put in front of the one who loved us so much that He died on our behalf, cleaning us so that we through His righteousness may come into the holy presence of God.

May we take time to seek Him and get direction on what things in our houses need to be cleaned out of them.

Have a blessed day.

Brother Mark

CHAPTER 4

22

CRIBBING

I APPLIED TO THE FIRE DEPARTMENT BECAUSE
I wanted a steady job that would take care of my family. I had no idea what the career really required. I did not grow up dreaming of being a firefighter. I simply envisioned hoses, axes, ladders and some pretty nice-looking trucks.

I had no idea about the diversity of services a firefighter was required to provide.

One of those was vehicle extrication. Removing a victim trapped in a vehicle after an accident.

I was privileged to have really good instructors in this discipline. We learned how to use cutters, spreaders, saws and other tools to safely make access to and remove those trapped inside.

The key was doing it in a manner that was safe for the victim and the firefighter.

The first thing we learned in all of this training was the importance of using "cribbing" to stabilize the vehicle so you could work safely on cutting into it.

Cribbing mostly consisted of various lengths of 4x4 and 2x4 boards.

These were most often placed under an unstable vehicle, regardless of whether it was on its wheels, its side, or its top, to keep it from moving around while the cutting and spreading operations were done to remove the occupant of the damaged car.

Cribbing was used to make the unstable stable, so someone in a bad situation could be helped. So someone who was perishing could be given the help they needed to be saved.

Synthetic cribbing is often used today. But in yesteryear the book taught that it should be maple, ash, or oak. These had the proper qualities needed to hold up the weight of a vehicle and not crack or slip easily.

We found that when the vehicle was properly "cribbed," or stabilized, the work could be done with much more confidence.

Stabilization.

In my life I have found myself damaged. Sometimes by my own actions and decisions, sometimes by the actions and decisions of others.

We all go through times when life makes us feel like we are rocking back and forth. Life doesn't feel stable. We need something to help us have confidence, assurance, and stability.

In these times, I see the grace of God so clearly. I see in His love for us that He always notices when we are damaged, unstable, and being rocked by the things of this world.

We need help and He shows up, and He applies the "cribbing." His is not maple, ash, or oak. His is comfort, understanding, compassion, peace, strength, and love. They give us confidence, assurance, and stability.

And He sent it in the gift we know as Jesus.

Because it was not pleasing to Him that anyone perish.

John 3:16-17

"For God so loved the world that He gave His only begotten Son, that whoever believes in Him should not perish but have everlasting life. For God did not send His Son into the world to condemn the world, but that the world through Him might be saved."

2 Corinthians 4:16

Therefore we do not lose heart. Even though our outward man is perishing, yet the inward man is being renewed day by day.

Always remember the "cribbing" available to you in Christ when life gets unstable. It is always available to us if we will just call out.

Brother Mark

23

GET UP AND COME ON WITH IT

WHEN I WAS SIXTEEN YEARS OLD, MY DAD HAD a massive stroke at the age of fifty-six. Until that time he had been a strong, energetic, take-control-and-get-it-done type of individual. Seeing him go from being that person to being partially paralyzed on his right side, with slurred speech and the need for a cane, came as a hard blow to my entire family.

But I learned that this man had a strength in him that surpassed his physical ability or obvious talents.

A few years later, I got myself into a bad place in life. I had lost direction and entered into a pit of hopelessness and self-pity. I had gone to spend some days at my parents' house and was doing little more than sitting around in a daze.

It was my third day there, and I had shared my frustrations with my dad the night before. He had asked me what I was going to do, in his very straightforward way. I had come up with some options of how I could maybe move on, and I shared those with him.

He responded, "Well, you will either do something or nothing. Nothing is a choice, but not a good one."

The next morning, I got out of bed and was just sitting in a chair, again debating where to go from this mess I had made of life and wanting to slip toward that hopeless mindset once again. Then I heard it, and I knew what it was. Thump, shuffle, thump. My dad was coming down the hall with his good step on the left leg followed by the shuffle of his bad leg and the thump of the cane.

My dad didn't knock on the door. He just opened it and asked, "Well?"

I just looked at him, not sure what he was asking.

"You said last night you needed to make a decision. What is it?" he asked.

I had to laugh a bit, but at that point I realized what he was doing. He was telling me it was time to stand up and move on.

That move on his part caused me to do what I needed to do, which was decide what direction I was going to go. In that moment, I decided, and stated what that decision was.

My dad looked at me for about ten seconds and then said something that has helped me my whole life.

"Well, get up and come on with it, then."

In other words: "It's time for action."

I then realized there was a faith and strength in this old man that you couldn't see from the outside.

My dad, who had come from a small farm in East Texas in the Depression era, gone through World War II, lived through severe burns from hot asphalt on 20 percent of his body while working a roofing job, now showed me it was his faith that had brought him through. All he had to do was trust God, get up, and come on with it.

As I prepared to get in my car that day, he called me back to the lawn chair he always sat in and said, "He will never leave you."

Two years later, I made my decision to put my trust in Jesus.

That night, I kept hearing something in my heart ask, "Well?"

When I chose to accept what Jesus offered, the phrase, "Well, get up and come on with it," came to my mind.

That day in my dad's house when I made my decision, I felt as though a burden had been lifted. I had made a decision.

That night in Jacksonville, Florida, "I got up and went on with it."

And the chains fell off. I remembered what Dad had said: "He will never leave you."

When life gets difficult, or when I have messed it up as much as I can and feel defeated, or I am heartbroken, I remember two very important things.

I need to remember that He has never left me and that my part is to get up in faith, and come on with it.

When we feel burdened and imprisoned by the things in this life, or maybe a decision we regret, let us remember that we are not alone when we have Christ, trust Him, and get up and get on with it in faith.

Acts 12:6-8

And when Herod was about to bring him out, that night Peter was sleeping, bound with two chains between two soldiers; and the guards before the door were keeping the prison. Now behold, an angel of the Lord stood by him, and a light shone in the prison; and he struck Peter on the side and raised him up, saying, "Arise quickly!" And his chains fell off his hands. Then the angel said to him, "Gird yourself and tie on your sandals"; and so he did. And he said to him, "Put on your garment and follow me."

May we never fall to hopelessness, because He knows where we are and will never leave us.

We only need to stand up, have faith and follow.

Get up and come on with it.

Brother Mark

24

WHEN CALLED

MANY YEARS AGO, DURING THE TIME MY WIFE and I were dating, we had made plans to go to dinner and a play in the neighboring town.

As we traveled the interstate, I saw multiple brake lights coming on ahead of me and knew I better catch the frontage road if I could, or we might not make it to our planned events of the evening. Fortunately, there was an off ramp there, so I quickly took it.

As we proceeded along, I looked down to the interstate highway and saw that a car had run headlong into a bridge pillar. It was in an area that I knew was a good distance away from any help arriving and there were multiple cars stopped. I could see one person lying on the ground and a group of people looking into the car, which made it obvious to me that someone was still inside.

I looked at my date. I looked at the clothes I had on. I thought about the plans we had.

Then I pulled over and told the lady who would one day be my wife that I felt I should go down to the accident.

I did, and there was a critically injured man on the ground and a man trapped in the wrecked vehicle.

I examined the man on the ground and asked other bystanders to stay by him to keep him calm. I then checked the man in the car and sized up situation.

I had no tools, and no medical gear other than a pair of medical gloves. I used a towel someone provided to try to stop some bleeding of the man in the vehicle.

This was long before cell phones were a common thing and I certainly did not have one, but someone did, and they had me talk to the 911 operator and explain the situation.

When the fire department and EMS did arrive, I identified myself as a firefighter and where I worked, expecting to get dismissed and ready to get out of their way.

But the captain on the ladder company asked my thoughts on the extrication process for the patient, probably out of professional courtesy. I wound up working with them until they got the man extricated from the vehicle.

I returned to my car, drenched in sweat, as it was a summer evening in Texas where sweating is a given condition if outside more than two minutes, especially if you are working. I had gotten dirty from kneeling by the vehicle, and the towel I had used to control bleeding had not controlled it all. I definitely needed to clean up.

I apologized to my date. We obviously could not continue with our plans.

She was completely supportive of my decision. Which I, of course, was glad of.

She told me, "That's what you do. I would have been more surprised if you had not stopped."

I and every other fire fighter have no doubt had the "off duty" experience several times. Never have I decided to *not* help anyone on the scene of an auto accident, or any other type of emergency, if there was a need for my help.

It's what we do. It's who we are.

I have been thinking about my service, both on and off duty through the years.

Again, I have never decided to pass an emergency because I was "off duty." I always felt like it was my duty, my responsibility, to serve people when the need presented itself.

I have also been thinking about my walk with Christ. My duty, my responsibility, my privilege, to serve Him.

I am proud of my profession and our commitment to serve.

I have been thinking about whether I was just as proud to be a servant of Christ, and if my commitment to serve Him was a strong as my commitment to my profession.

What I really began questioning myself about was: *Have I passed any event that Christ has put before me, where who I am as a follower of Christ would have been helpful?*

Have I passed a brother or sister firefighter who I knew was dealing with a "wreck" in their life?

Had I failed to share the lifesaving gospel of Christ with anyone I came across who evidently needed a word of love and encouragement?

Would I have cancelled plans for a date to comfort someone if Christ had put them before me?

I am quick to help with a rescue, but am I just as available to my Lord when He calls out for me to serve?

Or do I just do my church attendance and general religious functions and go "off call/off duty" the rest of the time?

Am I willing to be inconvenienced, uncomfortable? Am I willing to get dirty and sweaty?

Are my plans for life open to changes that Christ wants to make?

Matthew 16:24

Then Jesus told his disciples, "If anyone would come after me, let him <u>deny himself</u> and take up his cross and follow me."

That evening, I was willing to give up my time with my date, change my plans on the fly, get sweaty, and get a bit contaminated for the sake of helping someone, because that is what I do.

I pray that I am as available to Christ, even if He is calling me out of the comfort zone of "what I do."

I pray that I might be always willing to "be on call" for His Kingdom.

I have dedicated so much to the wonderful privilege of being a firefighter.

I pray my heart of service would be even stronger for His Glory.

Matthew 6:20-21

But lay up for yourselves treasures in heaven, where neither moth nor rust destroys and where thieves do not break in and steal. For where your treasure is, there your heart will be also.

As followers of Christ, it's what we do, it's who we are.

I pray that "when called" by Jesus, I will always hear and respond.

Stay safe and take care of each other.

Brother Mark

25

WHEN IT'S A WHISPER, AND NOT A SHOUT

AT THE FIRST WORKING FIRE I RESPONDED TO as a rookie, I was surprised by many things. I suppose that was natural, as it was my first experience in fighting a fire. I was surprised at how fast things moved, how the experienced firefighters worked so quickly and efficiently, the organization to the chaos, and I absolutely noticed how loud it was.

The sound of the fire as it burnt through the structure, fire pumps roaring, bystanders yelling, officers shouting orders, the horns and sirens of incoming apparatus. **Loud**.

As my officer shouted in his SCBA face piece, I found that if I listened, I could actually make out what he was saying. This was long before the face piece mounted enunciators. You had to shout loudly to be heard through the face piece.

I remember, especially when I was a rookie, the officer had to do a lot of yelling in his face piece to give me direction. I knew he was teaching me as well as keeping me safe, but I had to really be tuned in and listen so I could understand what he needed from me.

Shouting was also common inside the fire station. "You have a phone call!" "It's hot!" (Meaning supper was ready) Or just general poking fun at one another.

Loud and firefighting often went together.

But I have learned over the years that it is easy to hear the shouting, but if I care about others in my life, I need to listen for the whisper amidst the shouting.

Sometimes our brother firefighters are suffering, wrestling, struggling with things we encounter in the job, and sometimes the things we encounter in just leading our lives.

We will be the first to respond on scene if we hear "firefighter down." That radio traffic we never want to hear.

But we need to hear the quiet sounds that come from our brothers and sisters. That shift when they are withdrawn and saying little. Taking off on sick leave too often. Displaying emotions that are unusual. Or not displaying anything at all.

Just not being themselves.

If we saw someone in danger on any emergency incident, we would immediately shout out and take action to defend them.

We have reached a point where line of duty deaths are not the only things taking the lives of our brothers and sisters in high numbers each year. We are seeing lives lost, not only by the hazards of the emergency scene, but by a state of hopelessness. We have to listen for not only the shouting, but also be attentive to those quiet things our brothers and sisters may be telling and showing us.

And when we notice them, we have to do our best to show them we are standing with them.

Our people deal with a lot of things that other segments of our society never have to deal with. But at the same time, they have to deal with life as it happens. The same firefighter who experiences the multiple fatality may be facing family issues, financial hardship, addiction problems, or any of a hundred other things that all others deal with. Their plate can be full in a hurry.

Even with us trying our best, we cannot solve all of someone's struggles. But if we listen, and watch, and give as much care in their lives as we do on the emergency incident, we cannot help but make it better.

We are in times of great stress in our society right now.

Be attentive to the whispers of our brothers and sisters in the fire service, of our families and friends, and of our neighbors.

1 Corinthians 12:25-27

....but that the members should have the same care for one another. And if one member suffers, all the members suffer with it; or if one member is honored, all the members rejoice with it. Now you are the body of Christ, and members individually.

I pray I will listen, even for the whispers.

Brother Mark

26

THROWING LADDERS

LADDERS AND FIREFIGHTING GO TOGETHER.
They are so much a part of the job that ladders are
often a part of a fire department patch or logo.

From the time I entered the fire service, the
expression "throwing ladders" was used to describe
moving a ladder from the truck to an upright position where it was needed. The ladders are put in
place for several reasons. They allow a victim in
a structure to climb down, they allow a firefighter
who gets cut off from his exit to escape, and most
often, the ladder allows firefighters to move upward
and get in the place they need to be to make the
rescue or extinguish the fire.

In ladder training we found that moving up a
ladder to get the job done was difficult. When carrying the burden of a fire hose or other tools, it
could be challenging. But as we grew in experience and as we trained to prepare ourselves, we

found we became more efficient in throwing the ladder and moving up it. We grew in skill and in strength. This was expected of us, and we expected it of ourselves.

We knew the day would come when we needed to put this experience to work as we served one another and those who called on us for help.

I have come to realize that in my faith, in my service to God, I should be always growing in strength and moving upward.

I can just throw ladders, maybe invite someone to church service, tell them to "have a blessed day" or "I will pray for you." These are fine, but my Lord expects that I should be willing to move upward and take my faith to a higher place. Up the ladder of faith, carrying with me the tools of obedience, the love of God, compassion, and grace.

Throwing ladders is fine, but we should always be climbing in faith.

We must be prepared to go where we are needed in our service to God.

Sometimes the climb is difficult, but we should always be moving up in our faith. Status quo in our relationship and service to our Lord is not His calling.

May we always be moving upward in taking the gospel of Jesus to those who need it.

Philippians 3:12-14

Not that I have already attained, or am already perfected; but I press on, that I may lay hold of that for which Christ Jesus has also laid hold of me. Brethren, I do not count myself to have apprehended; but one thing I do, forgetting those things which are behind and reaching forward to those things which are ahead, I press toward the goal for the prize of the upward call of God in Christ Jesus.

I pray that we will always be climbing.

Brother Mark

27

WET BUNKERS

I ALWAYS NOTICED THAT IN THE DEPARTMENT where I spent the major part of my career, we had two terms for out firefighting personal protective apparel: "Bunker" and "Turn out" gear.

The history behind these names is very interesting. It is said that the volunteers in New York would sometimes sleep in the fire station in bunks. It was called "bunking." So when they got woke up for a fire, they would "turn out" of the bunk and would put on the firefighting clothing beside their bunk, "bunker gear" or "turnout gear," and respond.

Despite which name a person used for the gear, it was understood.

When you had your bunker gear fitted and worn in just right, it could be pretty comfortable overall. When it was dry.

But get the bunker gear wet, which of course happened regularly, the bunker gear quit being quite so comfortable. It just came with doing what you did.

Today, my firefighters have two sets of bunker gear. When one set is wet and contaminated from the fire, they get back to the station and switch into their extra set while the first set is being cleaned and dried.

Years ago this was not an option. You had one set to work with regardless of how many fires or accidents you might make in that shift. Being a firefighter in central Texas, the bunkers often got saturated just working a vehicle accident, due to the high temperatures and the fact that bunker gear much resembles wearing your grandmother's homemade quilt on your back while it is 102 degrees outside and you are doing patient care, extrication, or traffic control.

After getting back to the station and setting up our gear for the next call, we would point a fan on them, hoping it would help remove the moisture. It was a good thought but really did not help much.

Inevitably, when that gear got good and saturated, and we had cleaned up a bit and put on a dry pair of underwear, that tone would go off and we would have to slide back into those wet bunker pants. Not pleasant, very heavy from the added moisture, and they would bind up on us when we were pulling them on. Pretty nasty feeling.

I remember hurrying toward the truck and thinking, "Man, my fresh cloths are about to get soaked again." And that cold shock when the saturated gear that had a fan blowing on it was pulled up and put on.

Unpleasant, heavy, and actually dangerous to wear into another fire when it was wet, it just would not protect us like the dry gear would.

When the shift ended, we would break the bunker gear down by separating the inner and outer layers, hose it off and hang it to dry. If we had good firefighters working the following shift, they would rotate it around so it would dry thoroughly.

I recall one brother firefighter who forgot to rinse and hang his gear up at the end of the shift. He was tired, ready to get home, so he "stowed his gear wet." Forty-eight hours later, it was still wet, heavy, and smelled really bad.

It is important to make the effort, no matter how tired or in a hurry you are, to get those bunkers cleaned and dried out. Nobody wants to put those wet bunkers on.

As I look at life with over six decades behind me and thirty-five years in the fire service, I notice that in some ways I repeatedly put on "wet bunker gear."

Although I know I should address things in my life that repeatedly give me problems, I continue to "stow them away wet," and act surprised when I get the same unpleasant, heavy, or nasty results.

In other words, I continually make a choice to do the same thing over again, despite the fact that it makes life more difficult.

Sometimes this is a habit. And those are hard to break.

Sometimes it is an attitude toward something or somebody. Also tough to overcome at times.

Resentment is another set of "wet gear" we can jump into. Worry is a really heavy coat, as is regret. Trauma in our lives often saturates us and weighs us down over and over again.

Basically, spiritual, mental, and emotional "wet bunkers" not only feel bad and weigh us down, but they also put us at risk of more harm.

It was harder to fight fires when the bunkers got saturated.

It is also hard to live when our spirit and mind are weighed down.

The wet bunkers come from working the fire.

The spiritual, emotional and mental burdens come from living life.

Maybe the answer for either of these is having access to a clean set.

My firefighters today just shift into another dry and well fitted set. They have that option. If they did not exercise that option, it would be uncomfortable and dangerous.

We get tired in this life. It moves so fast and seems to demand so much: Family, career, expectations of others and ourselves. Sometimes we just want to "stow the gear wet," move on, and hope it is better when we get back to it. But it rarely is.

Truth is, we need a "change of bunker gear." We need to quit putting that heavy and unpleasant gear on again and again. It always has the same result. It just gets wetter. It just gets heavier. We get more tired, and sooner or later it seems to be too much to carry.

God has something new for us to put on in place of these heavy, unpleasant, and dangerous things we have been wearing over and over again. Something different from those repetitive efforts that bring the same poor and sometimes painful results.

Christ faced life in His time on earth. Just like us. He understood the demands, the challenges, and even the sadness that comes with living.

He made some promises and gave us some "new gear" to use.

Matthew 11:28-30

Come to Me, all you who labor and are heavy laden, and I will give you rest. Take My yoke upon you and learn from Me, for I am gentle and lowly in heart, and you will find rest for your souls. For My yoke is easy and My burden is light."

God promises that "His gear" is not heavy and the yoke indicates that He will be carrying it with you.

Again, we often return to our old and uncomfortable ways of thinking and living. Knowing the results, we "put them on" anyway because they are familiar and we don't know what else to do. God promises something new that will strengthen us and prepare us to move forward.

Ephesians 4:20-24

*But you have not so learned Christ, if indeed you have heard Him and have been taught by Him, as the truth is in Jesus: that you **put off**, concerning your former conduct, the old man which grows corrupt according to the deceitful lusts, 23 and be **renewed in the spirit of your mind**, and that you **put on***

*the new man which was created according
to God, in true righteousness and holiness.*

The faithfulness of God ensures us that we will always have a "fresh set" of protective gear to put on when we meet the demands, challenges and even the heartaches of life.

Matthew 28:20

*"and lo, I am with you always, even to the
end of the age." Amen*

May we always remember that we have that "new set of gear" available. We do not have to go back to what does not serve us well.

Psalm 59:16

*But I will sing of Your power;
Yes, I will sing aloud of Your **mercy** in
the **morning**;
For You have been my defense
And refuge in the day of my trouble.*

Watch out for yourselves and one another.

Brother Mark

28

SMOKING BEHIND THE PUMP HOUSE

MY PARENTS WERE BORN IN 1919 AND I CAME along as the seventh child when they were both near their fortieth birthdays. Growing up in the 60s and 70s, my parents made sure of one thing: When the church house doors were open, we were there.

In fact, my parents would drive the family fifty miles to attend a small country church in a farming area. That meant 100 miles as a round trip. We went Sunday morning and night as well as Wednesdays.

I wanted to attend a church in our town, but Dad said, "We are needed in that church body."

Very few kids attended but the preacher's son was about my age, and they were good days. As we reached the seventh grade, we both, of course, began to think of ourselves as being very cool and grown up.

In those days, many young boys thought that that picking up smoking was a crucial milestone in the journey toward being cool. I and the preacher's son were no different, and in the interlude between Sunday school and the worship service and during church fellowship gatherings, we took to having a smoke behind the church well pump house.

Cigarettes were easy to buy in those days, as you just told the store clerk you were picking them up for your dad.

We had many a good time, coughing as we looked so very cool, hiding behind a pump house behind a country church in the middle of nowhere.

One day on the ride home, my mom said she was disappointed that I was smoking, and especially disappointed that I would do it at church meeting.

I was stunned. At a loss for words, you might say.

My dad smoked, so I think that was why he did not dole out his usual stern disciplinary action upon me.

I sat there in the back seat asking myself, "How the heck did they know?" We were so well hidden. So secretive and careful that we were not seen.

I will never forget what my dad did say. He was driving and apparently able to guess what I was thinking. All he said was, "Smoke goes up."

Apparently, it was obvious what I and the preacher's son were doing, although we had no idea that our actions were being observed the entire time. While we thought we "hid" with our cigarettes, the smoke was rising from behind the pump house and my dad had seen it.

So many times in life, I have recalled that statement my Dad made: "Smoke goes up."

As I walk through life, making choices day to day on how I will love, forgive, have compassion for and patience with others, I must remember that "smoke goes up."

And others can see what is really going on with me.

Sure, I can put up a front, much like hiding behind a pump house, but the truth will rise up. And who and what I really am and how I live out my life will show itself. The smoke will rise and show it.

Each night as I examine the day behind me, my actions, words, motives and thoughts, I realize that those I encountered today got a view of what was important to me, the good and sometimes not so good.

And then I must turn my face up to God and remember that He has seen and heard it all.

Every thought, every action, every word and motive in my heart.

I say I love others and I love my Savior Jesus. If I want to please this God I love and love others as He has loved me, I should care enough to seek God in all that I think, do and say.

Even when I am behind the pump house, and I think no one sees.

What we do goes up. God surely knows, and if we are either sincere in loving God and others, or not, it will be apparent immediately to God and eventually to all those around us.

I pray "my smoke" will always rise up to show love over hate, patience over judgment, and compassion over selfishness.

May "my smoke" show the grace of God that is in me.

After all, God sees all our smoke, all the time, because it rises up before Him.

And it cannot be hidden.

Brother Mark

Psalm 139:1-12

O LORD, You have searched me
and known me.
You know my sitting down and my rising up;
You understand my thought afar off.
You comprehend my path and my lying down,

And are acquainted with all my ways.
For there is not a word on my tongue,
But behold, O LORD, You know it altogether.
You have hedged me behind and before,
And laid Your hand upon me.
Such knowledge is too wonderful for me;
It is high, I cannot attain it.
Where can I go from Your Spirit?
Or where can I flee from Your presence?
If I ascend into heaven, You are there;
If I make my bed in hell, behold, You are there.
If I take the wings of the morning,
And dwell in the uttermost parts of the sea,
Even there Your hand shall lead me,
And Your right hand shall hold me.
If I say, "Surely the darkness shall fall on me,"
Even the night shall be light about me;
Indeed, the darkness shall not hide from You,
But the night shines as the day;
The darkness and the light are both alike to You.

CHAPTER 5

FROM THE OLD HANDS

29

TRADITIONS

I HAVE ALWAYS APPRECIATED THE DEEP AND rich traditions of the American Fire Service. Everything, from how we do things on shift to how we lay a brother to rest.

It is all noble and glorious, as far as I am concerned.

However, I have found that it is not the firefighter who just observes and keeps the traditions, but rather that firefighter who has a deep heart and concern for fellow firefighters and those he responds to who keeps the true tradition.

It is easy to go through the steps of following the "rule of tradition." But a far grander thing are those individuals who have a heart that cares about what the tradition is based upon.

In the fire service we call that a "heart of brotherhood." Going beyond just the keeping of traditions. Being the true brother. And true brothers are built by experiencing true brotherhood.

And how does this work within our faith?

Do we traditionally do what's right because it is right that we do them and our hearts are led to do them?

Or do we think we are right because we keep traditions?

I have pondered these questions for a long time. I watch and listen to others. More importantly, I watch and listen to myself.

It appears to be relatively easy to keep traditions such as attending church meetings, giving to the church and those in need, and giving attention to religious events and days such as Easter Sunday.

Am I seeking to feel like I am right with God because I keep these traditions?

Or... am I making a tradition of doing these things because I have been made right only by the grace and mercy of God and I want to be obedient and thankful to Him and to grow closer to Him?

The Pharisees who so often attacked Jesus had many religious traditions, but Jesus said they were like "whitewashed tombstones." Looking good on the outside but pretty rotten on the inside.

Traditionally, doing what's right as shown us through the love and direction of God is a good thing.

Assuming I am right because I keep traditional practices is an empty thing.

I have come to the conclusion that it comes down to what is driving me.

Do I attend church meetings, help those in need, and show compassion and love to others because I love God and am thankful for what He has given me by grace and for who He is?

Or...

Do I do these things because I think they make me right with God and not because I am right with God through the gift of Jesus?

Am I driven by my *love* for God or my desire to *feel* like I am right with God?

In either case, it is easy tell in someone if we take a good look.

Especially if we take a good look at ourselves.

2 Corinthians 13:5

Examine yourselves as to whether you are in the faith. Test yourselves. Do you not know yourselves, that Jesus Christ is in you?—unless indeed you are disqualified.

30

GRAY EAGLES...

I ATTENDED A FUNERAL TODAY. MY FIRST battalion chief was laid to rest.

Over thirty-five years ago, he came by my station on my first duty shift. He welcomed me. He gave me advice. He made me understand that I was his firefighter.

I recall the confidence and comfort that gave me.

A great person, a great fire ground commander, a great firefighter.

At the funeral, I saw many firefighters from the past. It struck me that despite the years they had been retired, they remained great firefighters. I remembered them as strong, confident, courageous, and caring.

I remember the faces from when we worked, laughed, and lived the life of servants to a community.

They moved more slowly today. The hair and mustaches were gray where they used to not be.

And I thought of eagles. Though gray and moving more slowly, they carried with them a character founded in bravery and brotherhood.

Their love for one another was apparent. And the stories began to flow about this battalion chief we honored, and then about one another. Pride and joy sounded from each tale.

And for a moment... a perfect moment... these gray eagles soared together again.

I took a moment to thank God that I had the privilege of knowing them, of serving with them. Of living and flying with them.

Many of my brothers have passed from this life lately. I suppose that reflects my age.

It is my hope that when this time is over for us, that I see them in that place called heaven.

Their impact on my life has been tremendous.

I have been and am blessed.

I pray God's wind will forever be under their wings.

I pray that these gray eagles will not be forgotten. Their service, their brotherhood was and remains proud and valuable.

I am thankful for this day in which I was privileged to gather with these gray, but glorious eagles.

The time we served together went by far too quickly. But again, it has been glorious.

As Job of the Bible spoke of his days, "They pass by like swift ships, Like an eagle swooping on its prey." *(Job 9:26)*

So it has been. But I thank God for this company of eagles.

Isaiah 40:31

But those who wait on the LORD
Shall renew their strength;
They shall mount up with wings like eagles,
They shall run and not be weary,
They shall walk and not faint.

Isaiah 43:2

When you pass through the waters, I will be with you;
And through the rivers, they shall not overflow you.
When you walk through the fire, you shall not be burned,
Nor shall the flame scorch you.

Brother Mark

31

ZERO VISIBILITY

AS I GET OLDER, I REMINISCE AS OLDER PEOPLE do. I was speaking with another old firefighter recently and we got on the subject of the many different fires we made where we experienced working in zero visibility and the feeling we sometimes got when we absolutely could not tell which way we should go from where we were. Being in a place like that really made us think about the training we received for dealing with those situations. I was fortunate, I think, to have been given good training throughout my career.

I started thinking about what it would be like to be in the zero-visibility environment without having taken the time to have been trained in dealing with it.

I then realized that at one point my life, I was in a zero-visibility environment mentally and spiritually. I was in a very dark place, and I could not see my way out of it.

When fighting fire and finding myself where I could not see where I should go, I remember that more than once I got a glimpse of light coming through a window or door, or I heard something that helped orient me, like another crew making their way through the structure. I remember that either the glimpse of light or the sound of a voice produced an assurance in me that I was in fact going to make my way out.

When experiencing the mental and spiritual zero visibility, the same thing holds true. If you could just see something that could comfort and direct you, it would be a great relief.

At a time in my life when alcoholism and despair had gotten me in a very dark place and it was difficult to imagine that I could recover from it, I began to feel a very terrible thing called hopelessness.

The old saying, "I could feel the devil walking next to me," was becoming a reality.

The enemy works hard to make us believe there is no hope. When he can do that, he wins over us.

In that dark, zero-visibility place I was in, a glimmer broke through and then a voice spoke to me. I know now it was God who loves me, who spoke to me in those times and assured me I was not alone and there was a light to follow out of the darkness. And that light was Him.

Too many times I have worked incidents or had someone I care about reach that point where they believe there is no hope.

I have lost some brother firefighters to that darkness.

God told us He had the solution for zero visibility. All it requires is that we look and listen. Look for the light and listen for His voice.

In Jesus there is not a place called hopeless. Only hope.

If you feel things getting dark around you and you cannot see your way out, remember Him who is the light of the world. Your hopelessness will be washed away by His light and His strong and gentle voice.

Brother Mark

Psalm 107:13-15

Then they cried out to the LORD in their trouble, and He saved them out of their distresses. He brought them out of darkness and the shadow of death, And broke their chains in pieces. Oh, that men would give thanks to the LORD for His goodness, And for His wonderful works to the children of men!